Rough Country Trading Post
P. O. Box 127
Dinosaur, Colorado 81610.
Wagner, John

Beauty of Sand Wash Basin
2nd edition, March 13, 2015

Book design by John Wagner
Photographs by John Wagner

More adventures by John Wagner

First Flight- Journey of a Man and an Eagle

The Magnificent Wild Mustangs of Sand Wash Basin

Picasso: Wild Stallion of the West

The Bird Herd of Sand Wash Basin

Fighting Stallions of Sand Wash Basin

Frightfull Freefall's Photo Album

Foxy Foxes

Rock Art & Ruins of Northwestern Colorado and Northeastern Utah

Corona, the Golden Boy and His Band

Hilarious Horses

Wild Horses of Sand Wash Basin

The Little Sacred Horses of Sand Wash Basin

Before you began your adventure to Sand Wash Basin, make sure you stop at the BLM Office in Craig, Colorado and buy a good map. Sand Wash Basin is laced with old seismograph trails, and if you're lucky, the wild horses you have spotted will be near one of these trails.

Also, be sure to stop at the Moffat County Tourism Association. It is located behind the Village Inn in the Centennial Mall in Craig, Colorado on West Victory Way (US40). For more information call 1-866-332-8436.

Once inside, you will see an 8x8 foot photo I did of a running band of wild horses. Melody Villard, director, has done an amazing job of showing the wonderful sites of Moffat County. Tell them that John Wagner from Dinosaur sent you. They have maps and displays, and the staff is awesome.

There is No Services Available in Sand Wash Basin!

Make sure your vehicle is full of gas, and the spare tire is aired up. The sharp flint type rocks can ruin a trip without a spare. Make sure your vehicle has a jack & tools to change a tire with!

Take plenty of drinking water, food, and bug repellent and include a First Aid Kit. Also include a warm jacket or coat. When the sun goes down the temp drops fast.

Sand Wash Basin lies in Northwestern Colorado. This is where the wild horses roam on 160,000 acres of BLM, state and private land. A variety of animals and birds call this place home too.

This high desert land is beautiful from Barren Badlands to Utah Juniper Trees. If you go to Sand Wash Basin bring a pair of binoculars so you can watch the wildlife; like the Burrowing Owls, Prairie Dogs, Hawks, Eagles, Thirteen-Lined Squirrels, and of course the Wild Mustangs.

The area is so huge that sometimes small bands of wild horses are hard to find. I've talked to different people that said, "We drove all day and only found one horse!" "Where are they hiding at?"

I smile and say. "Playing Hide & Seek."

Happy Trails
John

Beauty of Sand Wash Basin

by John Wagner

The Entrance to Sand Wash Basin off of Highway 318.

Burrowing Owls live in Prairie Dog holes. Most books say they live in abandon prairie dog holes. But these Owls have never read the book and they live with them!

Watch where you step!

"I have a Family of Woos that lives with Me." replied Diggy the
Prairie Dog.

Sage Grouse

"Look Mom. It's a Baby Dinosaur!
This is a Horned Lizard, also known as a Horny Toad!

Looking towards the Badlands.

Little Snake River from County Road 75.

I was sitting in my Van and it was raining cats & dogs. After the rain stopped, The Lord blessed it with a rainbow.

Two Stallions Fighting

Heading for the waterhole

Sunset Horses

Mule Deer

Looking to the South from County Road 48.

Looking North from County Road 48.

This landmark is called "Monument Hill."

Sand Wash Basin is a Rock hound Paradise. Petrified wood, algae, agates, jasper, chert and many other stones can be found in this area.

On the road again!

Two Bull Elk near Sheepherders Spring.

Red Fox hunting for food.

"Whoooo, are you?"

A touch of white.

Strawberry Cactus.

Picasso's Hoof-Print.

Watching over his domain.

Flight of Three Owls.

Benson with Demi peeking over his back.

Mountain Bluebird perched on Greasewood branch.

The Solar Pump keeps Lake Draw Pond full of water.

Looking Northeast from County Road 48.

I'll be watching for you!

John Wagner lives in Dinosaur, Colorado with his wife Sarah, daughter Megan and their dog Buddy. John loves the great outdoors and photography is his hobby.

www.ingramcontent.com/pod-product-compliance
Lightning Source LLC
Chambersburg PA
CBHW041524280526
45792CB00004B/1376